PROPERTY OF WAYNE COUNTY
INTERMEDIATE SCHOOL DISTRICT
CHAPTER 2, P.L. 97-35

GESU SCHOOL LIBRARY
DETROIT, MI 48221

SUN AND LIGHT

Neil Ardley

Series consultant: Professor Eric Laithwaite

Franklin Watts
London   New York   Toronto   Sydney

The author
Neil Ardley gained a degree in science and worked as a research chemist and patent agent before entering publishing. He is now a full-time writer and is the author of more than fifty information books on science, natural history and music.

The consultant
Eric Laithwaite is Professor of Heavy Electrical Engineering at Imperial College, London. A well-known television personality and broadcaster, he is best known for his inventions on linear motors.

© 1983 Franklin Watts Ltd

First published in Great Britain in 1983 by
Franklin Watts Ltd
12a Golden Square
London W1

First published in the United States of America by
Franklin Watts Inc.
387 Park Avenue South
New York
N.Y. 10016

Printed in Belgium

UK edition:
ISBN 0 86313 024 0
US edition:
ISBN 0-531-04616-8
Library of Congress
Catalog Card Number:
82-62992

Designed by
David Jefferis

Illustrated by
Janos Marffy,
Hayward Art Group and
Arthur Tims

SUN AND LIGHT

Contents

Equipment	4
Introduction	5
The Sun	6
Time and direction	8
Light rays	10
Mirror images	12
Strange reflections	14
Bending light	16
Magnifying power	18
Cameras and projectors	20
Colors in light	22
Color mixtures	24
Stop-go pictures	26
Strange effects of light	28
Glossary	30
Index	32

Equipment

In addition to a few everyday items, you will need the following equipment to carry out the activities in this book.

Telescope or binoculars
Two flat mirrors
Silver foil
Black marker
Protractor
Glass bowl
Three flashlights
Clear plastic bottle and flexible tube

Deep shiny spoon
Candle
Two magnifying glasses
Plastic strip
Two cardboard tubes
Table lamp
Red, green and blue clear plastic
Two pairs of polarizing sunglasses

Introduction

When we are born, we emerge from a realm of darkness into the light. During our lives, we are ruled by the Sun and its light as it governs time, dividing day from night and season from season. Light allows us to see the world in which we live, and the colors in light give it great beauty.

By doing the activities in this book, you'll find out how light behaves, how we see things, how we can use mirrors and lenses, how color works, and how light can produce strange kinds of images. There are also some entertaining tricks, like making a coin appear to float, and some interesting projects, such as making a sundial.

Take care when doing the activities, as several involve handling glass mirrors and lenses. Some require a candle flame as a source of light. Be careful not to burn yourself and make sure to blow out matches and candles afterwards.

✺ This symbol appears throughout the book. It shows you where to find the scientific explanation for the results of the experiment.

The Sun

Observe the Sun safely and see the power of its rays.

△ Project the Sun's image on the ceiling with a mirror as shown. You may need to focus and support the telescope or binoculars to get a sharp and steady image. You may also be able to see the spots that usually mark the Sun's face.

Sunwatch
Draw all the curtains. Place a telescope or one half of a pair of binoculars in a gap in the curtains so that the large end points *directly* at the Sun. The telescope or binoculars produce a big image of the Sun.

☀ The Sun's rays contain heat as well as light. You must **never** look at the Sun through a lens or a telescope or binoculars. If you do, the heat will damage your eyes. Always use this method to observe the Sun.

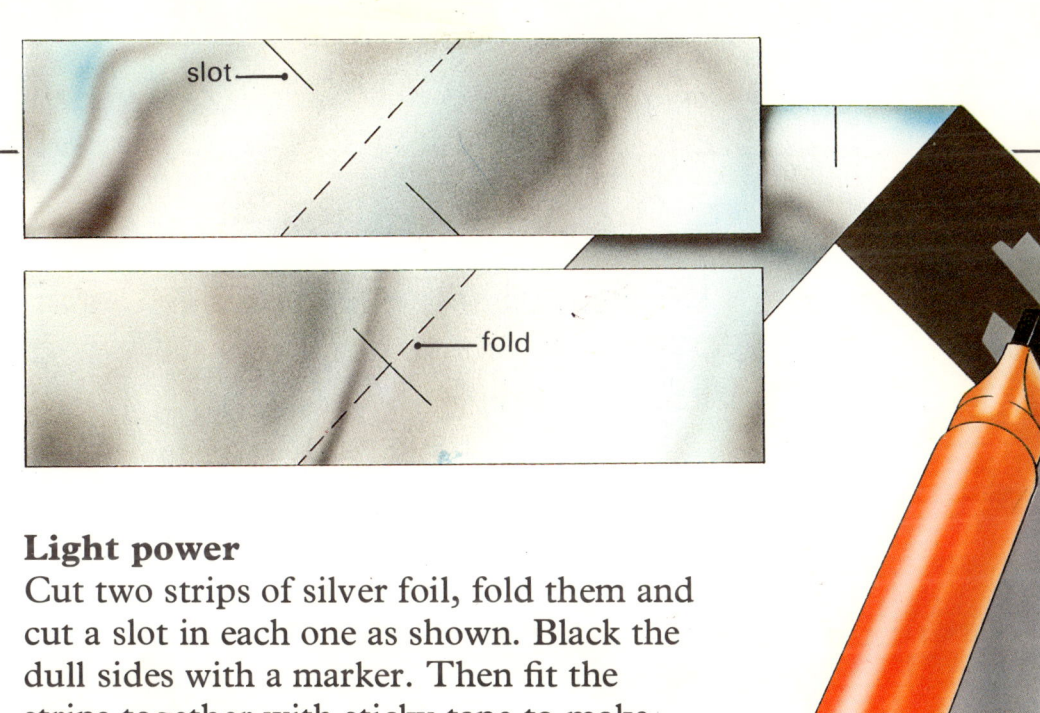

Light power

Cut two strips of silver foil, fold them and cut a slot in each one as shown. Black the dull sides with a marker. Then fit the strips together with sticky tape to make four vanes with shiny and black sides. Hang the vanes by a thread in a jar, cover the jar and place it in the Sun. The vanes slowly rotate in the light.

💥 Heat rays in the light move the vanes. They warm the black sides, which heat the air so that it pushes the vanes.

Time and direction

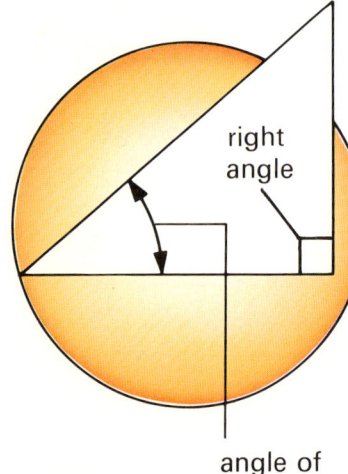

△ Find the angle of latitude of your home from an atlas. Use a protractor to mark out the triangle first.

Use the Sun as a clock and a compass.

Make a sundial
Cut a triangle from a piece of wood so that one angle is a right angle and another is equal to the angle of latitude. Glue the triangle to a board as shown. Draw in the lines marked 12. Mount the board in the Sun so that the shadow of the triangle touches the 12 o'clock lines at noon. Then, each hour, draw in lines marking the shadow for the other hours.

This sundial works throughout the year because the Sun, whether high or low, is always in the same direction at the same time of day. However, you may have to adjust an hour for Daylight Savings Time.

▽ The position of the edge of the shadow indicates the time.

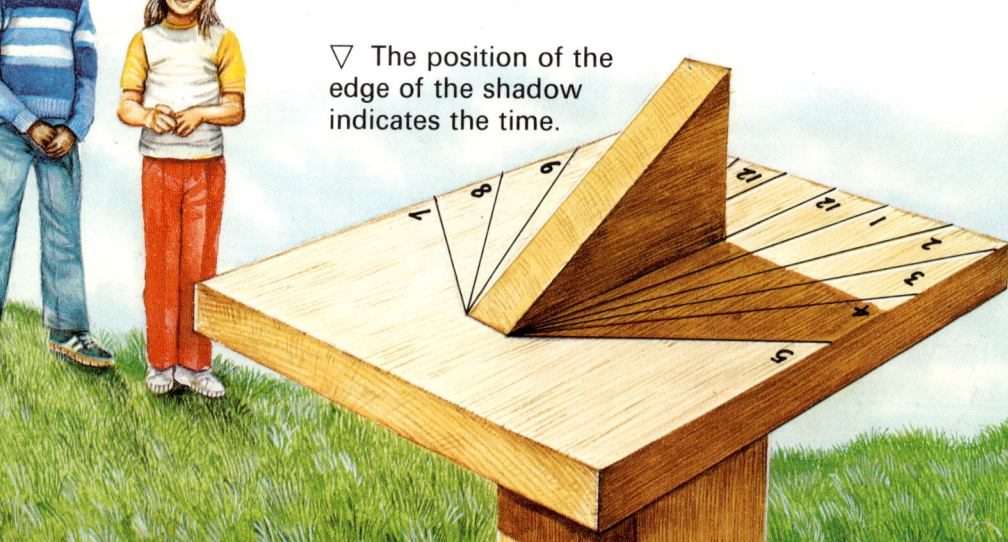

Sun compass

You can find your direction without a compass if the Sun is out. Draw a clock face on some paper, look at your watch and draw in the hour line as shown. Next draw a line from the center to 12, and then draw a line *exactly* halfway between the hour line and the 12 line. (If it is Daylight Savings Time, use 1 instead of 12.) Mark the halfway line South, and draw in the other directions as shown. Point the hour line at the Sun and the directions will be correct.

※ This Sun compass works because the Sun moves through the sky from east to west at the same speed every day. Its direction depends on the time of day.

△ In the southern hemisphere, point 12 at the Sun and mark the halfway line North.

▽ This is how to draw the lines at times before noon (am) and after (pm).

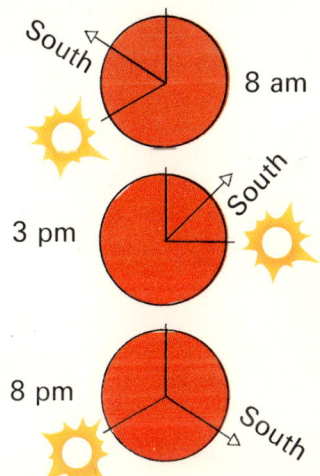

Light rays

See how light travels from one place to another.

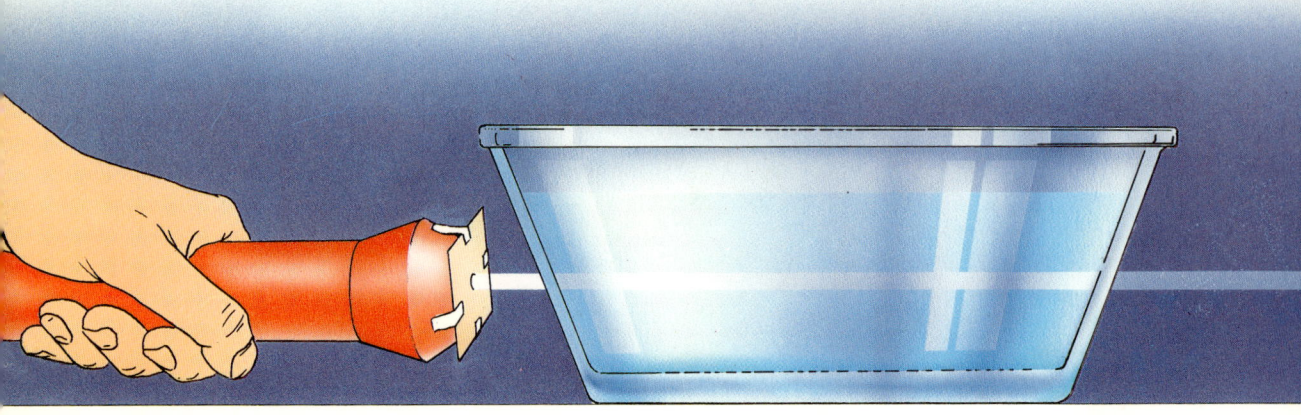

△ Place a small, flat mirror in the water to reflect the beam. Swivel the mirror and see how the reflected beam moves but always remains straight.

Ray display
Take a large glass bowl and fill it with water. Now add a few drops of milk and stir the water so that it turns a pale milky blue-white. Next tape a piece of card with a small hole in it over the end of a flashlight. Shine the flashlight through the side of the bowl, and you will see a straight beam of light in the water. The beam shows up best if it is dark.

✺ Light is made of rays that always travel in straight lines from one place to another. The rays are invisible in pure air or water. The droplets of milk in the milky water light up as the light rays strike them.

Light trap
Take a clear plastic bottle and a clear flexible tube. Make a hole in the lid of the bottle and push in the tube so that it fits tightly. Fill the bottle with water, place a flashlight under it and wrap them up in a heavy towel. Take this into a darkened bathroom and place the tube in the wash basin. Squeeze the bottle so that water comes out of the tube in a jet. You will see that light is carried along the tube and jet of water, producing a splash of light on the side of the basin.

✳ The light rays may seem to bend in the plastic tube and water jet. In fact, they are reflected to and fro by the inside surfaces of the tube and jet. The rays are still straight but are trapped inside the tube and jet.

△ The water jet carries light as long as it flows without a break.

Mirror images

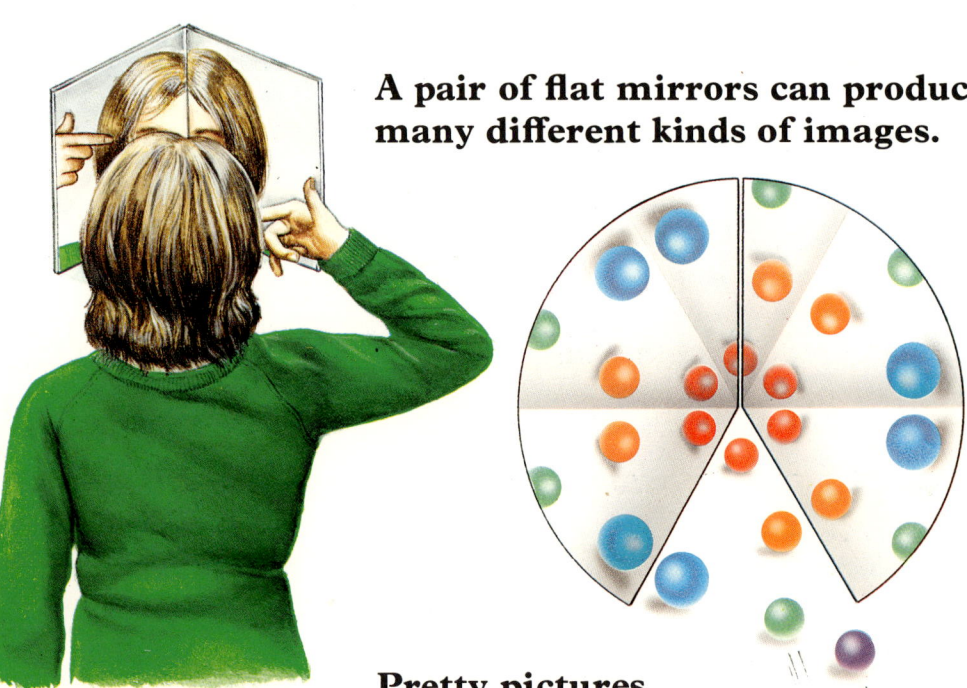

A pair of flat mirrors can produce many different kinds of images.

△ When you look in one mirror, the light rays from your face strike the mirror and are reflected back to your eyes. The image of your face is reversed. With two mirrors at a right angle, the rays are reflected by both mirrors. One mirror reverses the reversed image formed by the other mirror, making your face look the right way round. At a smaller angle, as in the kaleidoscope, the rays are reflected more times and give several images.

Pretty pictures
Take two flat mirrors that are the same size. Use sticky tape to fasten them together and stand the mirrors so that they are at a right angle. Look into the mirrors and touch your ear. Your image is the right way round. Now move the mirrors closer together and throw some colored beads between them. This is a kaleidoscope.

💥 The images in the mirrors are unusual because light rays are reflected between the mirrors before they go to the eye. In a kaleidoscope the mirrors give several images in a circular pattern.

Make a periscope

You can use a periscope to look around corners and over walls without being seen. You need two flat mirrors to make the periscope. Take a long, thin cardboard box, and cut holes as big as the mirrors in each end as shown. Next tape the mirrors into position in each end of the box so that they are at an angle of 45 degrees to the sides. The periscope is now ready for use.

💥 The two mirrors reflect light rays from an object down the periscope and into your eyes. You see the object in the bottom mirror, so it appears to be on the same level as you are.

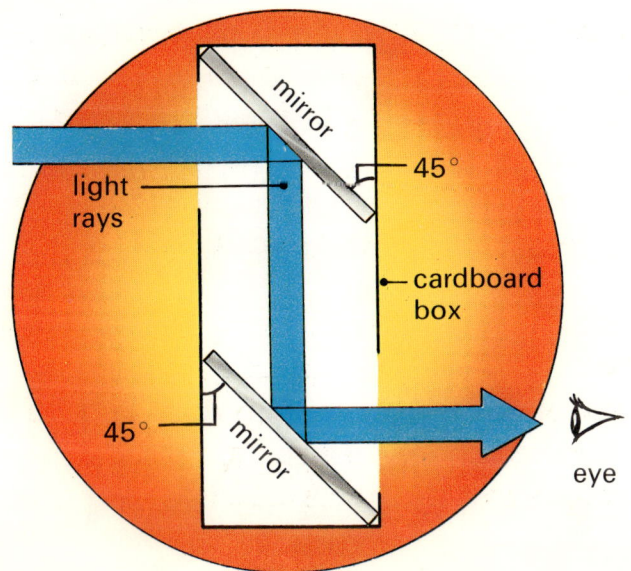

◁ This is how light rays travel down a periscope to the eyes. To get the mirrors at 45°, make sure that the distances from the edges of each mirror to the corner of the box behind the mirror are the same.

13

Strange reflections

Curved mirrors make everything look unusual.

△ Like the spoons shown here, some mirrors at amusement parks have surfaces that curve in and out to give funny images of people who stand in front of them.

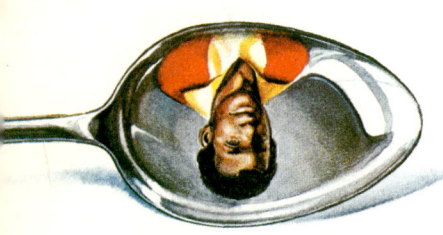

Shiny spoon

A shiny spoon with a deep bowl makes a good curved mirror. Look into the back of the spoon and see what a large nose you have. Now turn the spoon over and look into the bowl of the spoon. This time you're upside down! Close one eye and put the bowl of the spoon very close to the other eye. You see your eye enormously magnified.

💥 Curved mirrors give strange images because the different parts of the mirror reflect light rays at different angles.

14

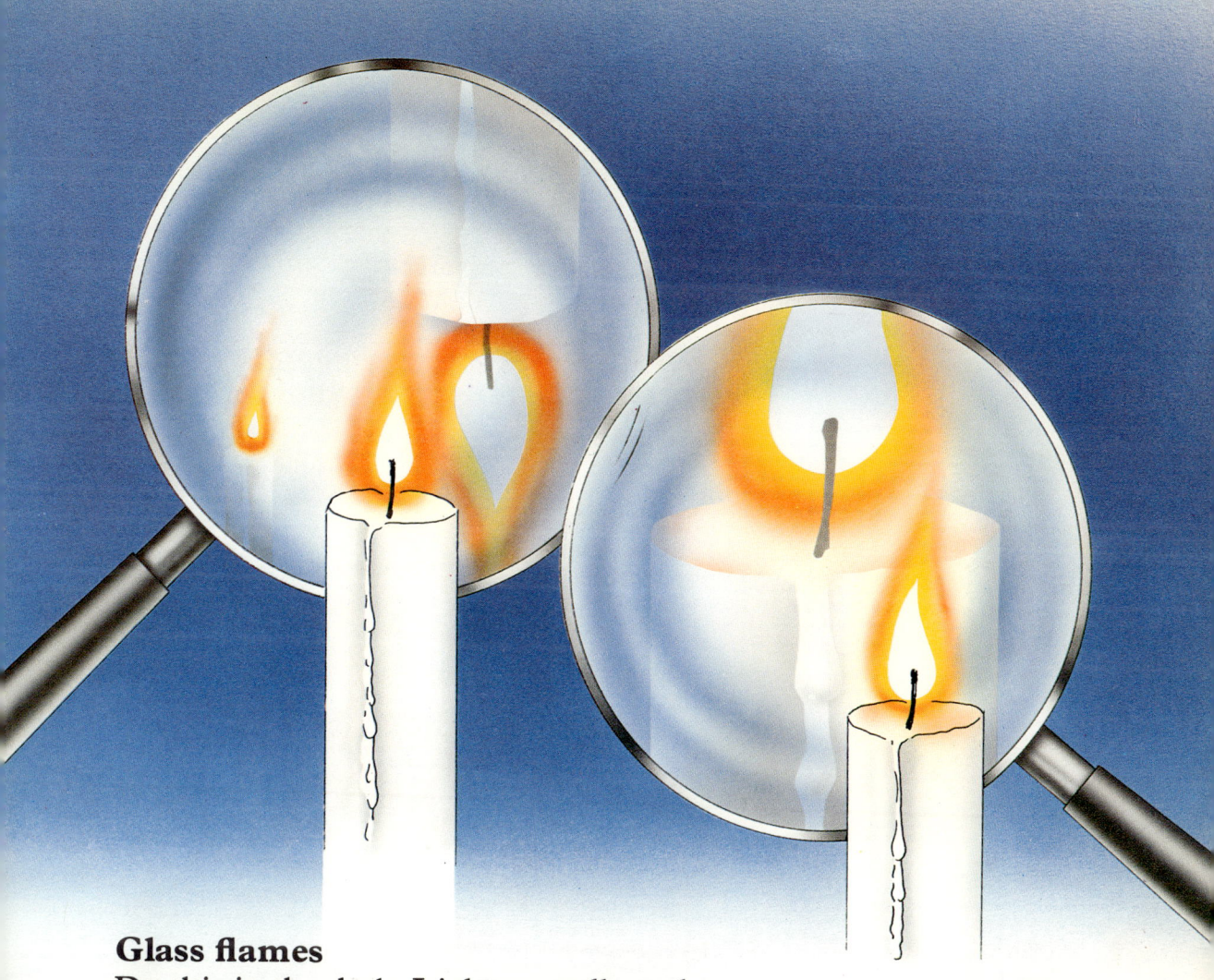

Glass flames

Do this in the dark. Light a candle and hold a strong magnifying glass about 4 in behind the flame. Look toward the candle and into the glass. You see two images of the flame, one small and upright, the other bigger and upside down. Bring the glass very near the flame. Now the upside-down flame is upright and huge.

✸ The flame is reflected in both the front and the back surfaces of the glass. These act like two curved mirrors to give two images.

△ The front surface of the glass curves out toward you. It always gives a small upright image of the candle flame. The back surface of the glass curves in, giving a huge upright image when it is near the flame and a smaller upside-down image farther away.

Bending light

See how light may bend as it goes from one substance into another.

△ You see an object whenever light rays from it strike your eyes. When you pour water into the glass, light rays from the coin bend at the water surface toward your eyes. You then see the coin at the surface of the water. When you take the book away, light also comes from the coin to your eyes through the side of the glass and you can also see the coin on the bottom.

Double your money

Put a coin into an empty glass. Then place a book in front of the glass to hide the coin. Tell your friends that, without touching the coin or glass, you can make the coin float and then double your money. To do this, slowly pour some water into the glass. The coin is seen to float. Take away the book, and you see two coins.

✹ Light rays bend as they pass from the water into the air. This makes the coin both appear to float on the water and lie on the bottom.

Seeing the light

You can show how light bends at a surface with the bowl of milky water and flashlight described on page 10. Shine the beam on the water at an angle. See how it changes direction as it enters the water.

※ This bending of light is called refraction. It happens when light rays enter or leave a transparent substance at certain angles. Light makes this change of direction when it goes from water into air. This is why the coin trick on page 16 works.

△ This works best in the dark. Smoke from a candle helps to show up the flashlight beam in the air.

▽ Lenses bend light rays by refraction. You can see this by using a magnifying glass to beam the Sun's rays into the bowl. The curved surfaces of the lens bend the rays so that they meet and then spread out again.

17

Magnifying power

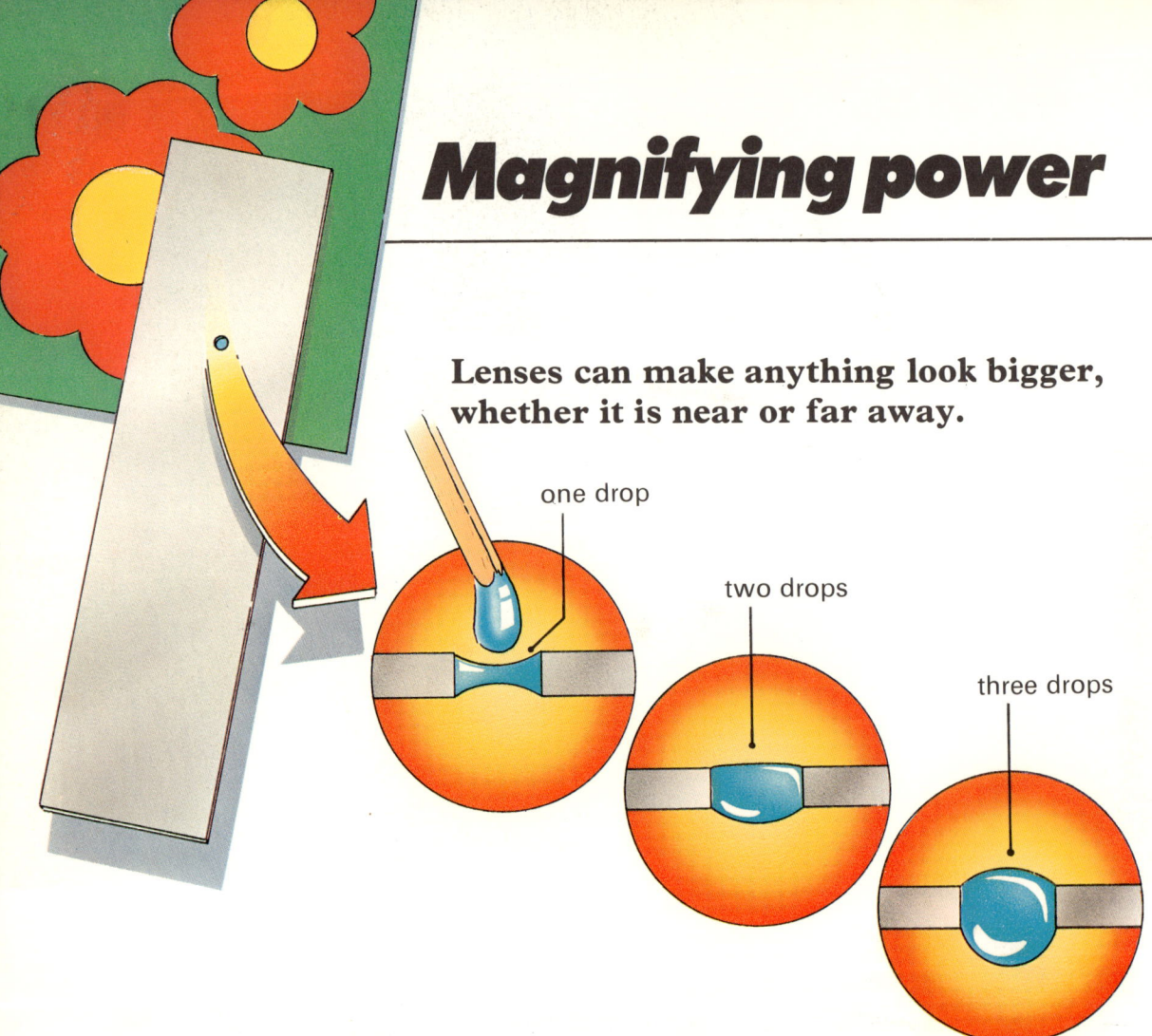

Lenses can make anything look bigger, whether it is near or far away.

one drop

two drops

three drops

△ You may need to use two or three drops of water to get high magnifying power. The water evaporates quickly, so you may need to add some more drops later.

Miniature microscope
Take a plastic strip $\frac{1}{25}$ in thick and make a hole in it about $\frac{1}{6}$ in wide. With a matchstick, place a drop of water in the hole. Hold the strip close to a printed color picture and look through the hole to get a magnified view.

✺ Lenses form images because they have curved surfaces. The sides of the droplet are highly curved, making it into a lens like a very strong magnifying glass.

Simple telescope

Take two magnifying glasses and two cardboard tubes. Fit one tube inside the other and tape one of the glass lenses to one end. Hold the second lens at the other end to make a telescope and look through it. Adjust the tubes and lens until you get a sharp magnified image. The image is upside down, but you can use this telescope to observe the Moon.

✺ The second lens forms an upside-down image of the Moon inside the tube. The first lens magnifies this image so that the Moon looks bigger.

△ The lenses inside telescopes, binoculars and microscopes bend the light rays coming from an object. They bend them so much that the rays arrive at the eye as if they had come from the same object placed nearer to the eye. This makes the object look nearer and therefore bigger.

19

Cameras and projectors

Make an image of an object appear on a screen.

△ To build this pinhole camera, make a tiny hole with a pin in one side of a cardboard box. Cut a large square hole in the opposite side, and tape a piece of tissue paper firmly over the hole.

Pinhole camera

Make a pinhole camera as described in the caption. In the dark, place a flashlight against the pinhole and look at the tissue screen. A large image of the bright filament in the flashlight bulb can be seen there.

✸ Light rays from the filament pass through the pinhole and form an image on the tissue screen. For this to happen, the hole has to be very small. You can put film

into a pinhole camera and take a picture, but the image is so faint that it needs a long exposure. A real camera has a lens to produce a brighter image on the film.

Primitive projector
Place a magnifying glass near the bulb of a table lamp. You can project a large image of the bulb on a screen or wall.

✹ The lens bends light rays from the bulb to form an image. The image is large if the lens is near the bulb. Film and slide projectors produce large pictures on a screen in the same way.

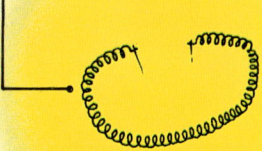

image of filament in bulb

▽ If you move the lens near the screen, you will form a small image of the lamp. The lens in a camera produces an image on the film in this way. The image is upside down and back to front.

21

Colors in light

Make colors from white light and put colors together.

△ Allow the water to become still to see the spectrum. You may need to put a coin in the dish to prop up the mirror.

▽ Sunlight passing into and out of raindrops makes a rainbow form in the sky.

Simple spectrum

Do this experiment when the Sun is low in the sky and shining through a window. Place a shallow dish of water in the sunlight. Then put a mirror in the water so that it faces the Sun as shown. A rainbow pattern of colors appears on the ceiling.

✸ White light such as sunlight is made up of several colors mixed together. As the light enters and leaves the water after being reflected by the mirror, the rays bend. Blue rays bend more than red rays, splitting the white light into a pattern of colors called a spectrum. A rainbow is a spectrum of sunlight.

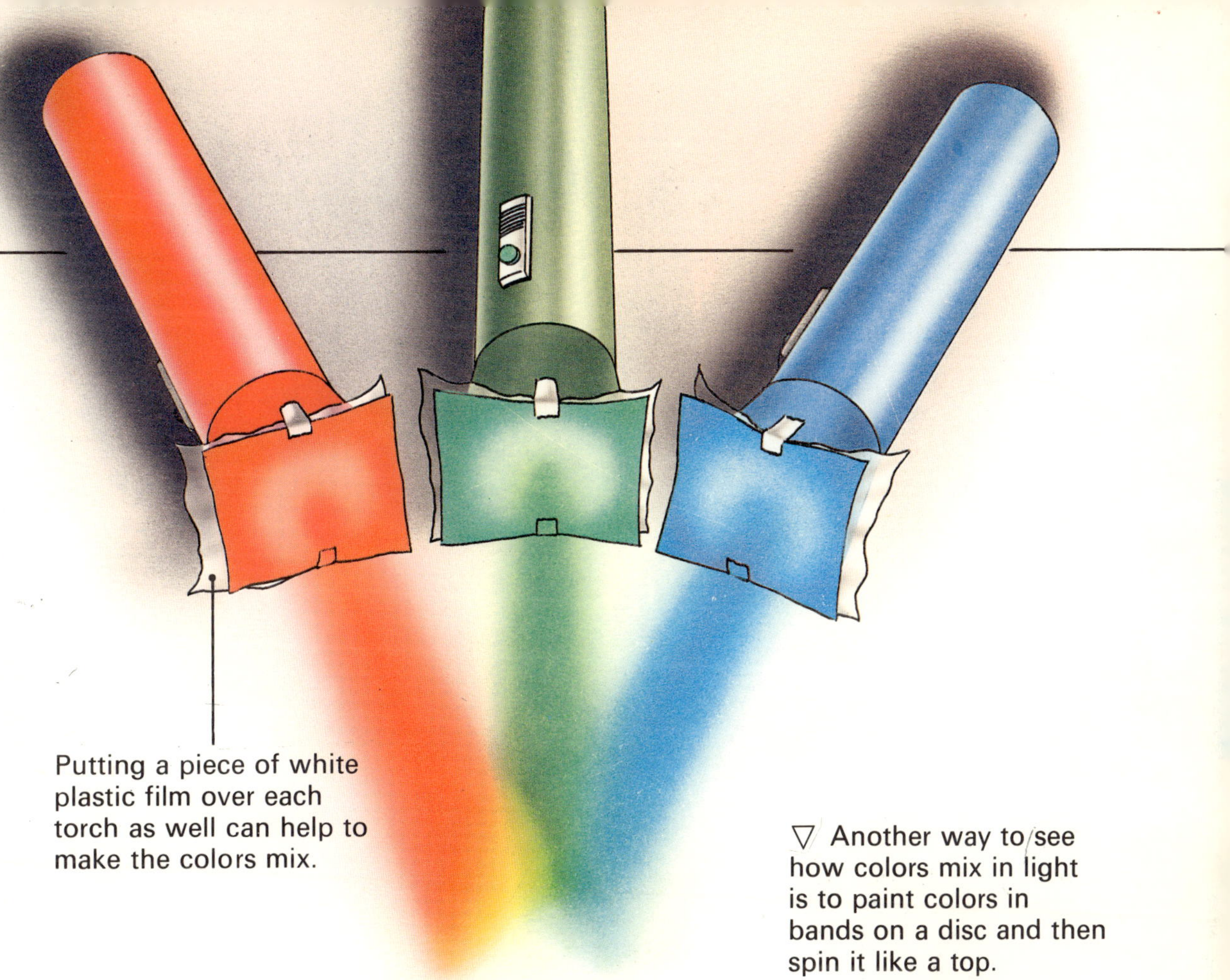

Putting a piece of white plastic film over each torch as well can help to make the colors mix.

Three colors only

Take three flashlights and fasten clear red, green and blue plastic over them. In the dark, shine patches of colored light on a white card. See how the colors mix to make other colors. Red and green make yellow. All three colors mix equally to make white.

💥 Every color that we see is a mixture of red, green and blue in the light that strikes our eyes. However, paint colors mix in a different way to colored lights. This is because paints change the color of the light before it reaches the eyes.

▽ Another way to see how colors mix in light is to paint colors in bands on a disc and then spin it like a top.

23

Color mixtures

Many colors are formed by taking other colors away from white light.

Sky colors
Take the glass bowl of milky water described on page 10. In the dark, shine a flashlight on the water from above. The water looks blue-white. Now shine the light through the water as shown. It looks orange-red from the other side of the bowl.

▽ When the Sun is low in the sky, the air takes blue and green from the rays, leaving only red.

✹ The milky water looks slightly blue because it takes blue from the white light of the flashlight. The air takes some blue from sunlight as the Sun's rays pass through it. This is why the sky is blue. The flashlight looks orange-red because only orange-red light passes through the water. The Sun is red at sunset and sunrise for this reason.

Use black ink, not pencil or crayon.

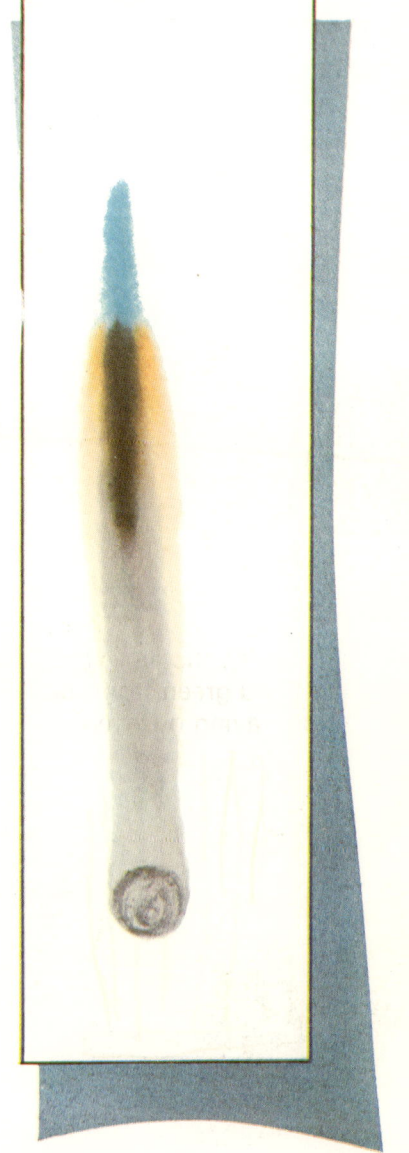

How black is black?

Mark a black circle on a thin strip of tissue paper. Hang the strip up with the end in a glass of water. The circle should be just above the water. Colors spread out of the ink and up the strip as it gets wet.

✸ This shows that the black ink is made up of several colored inks mixed together. Each ink takes away some color from the white light with which we see the paper. All the inks act together to take away all the colors from the light. As no colors are left, the ink looks black.

Stop-go pictures

Still pictures can appear to move and moving pictures appear to stop.

Flick trick
Draw a picture on one half of a paper strip. Fold it in two and draw another picture on the other half. Roll the top half around a pencil, then flick the pencil quickly to and fro. You see both pictures together.

💥 Your eyes view each picture separately for an instant, but the pictures remain in your brain for a slightly longer time. This is why they overlap. In films and television, you see many still pictures one after the other. They overlap in the same way so that they appear to move.

Waving hand and wagon wheel

Wave your hand quickly to and fro in front of a television screen. It appears to have many more fingers! Now draw a wagon wheel like that on the right and make a top. Spin the top in front of the screen. The spokes appear to turn slowly or even stop.

✸ The television picture in fact goes on and off many times a second. It lights up your hand or the top for an instant, forming still images in the eye. Your brain retains the images for a short time, overlapping them to give these effects.

△ Copy this pattern on to a piece of card to make a top. Like the top, moving wheels in films and on television often appear to turn slowly, stop or even go backwards.

Strange effects of light

Light passing through certain materials can behave strangely.

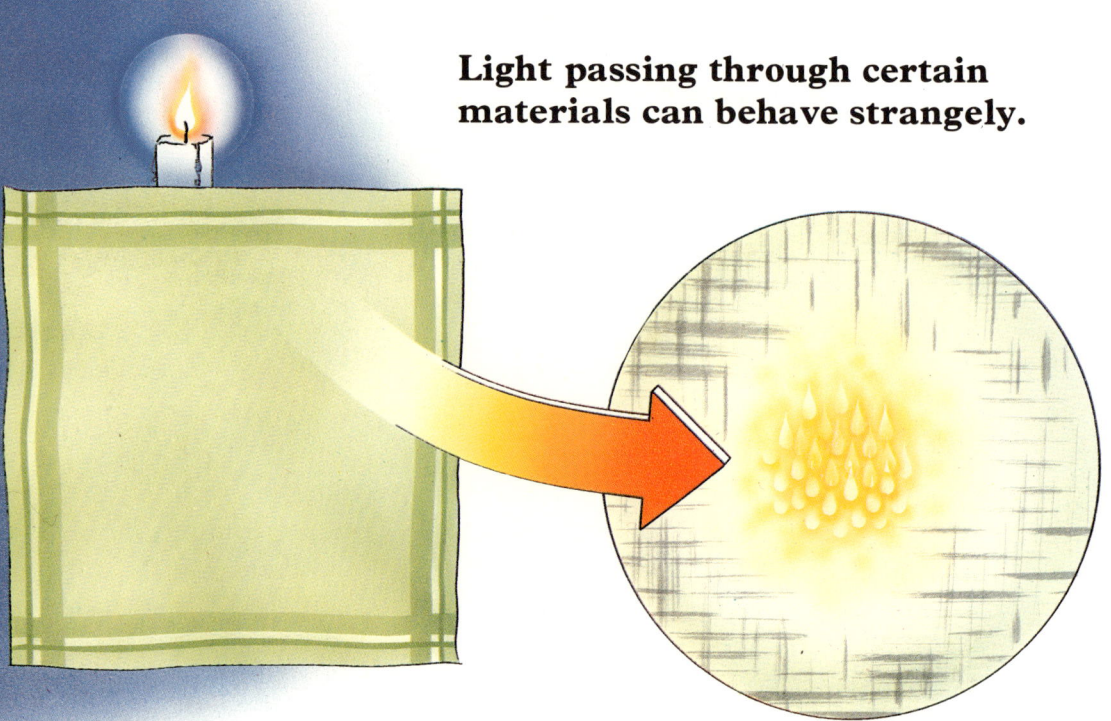

△ This effect is called diffraction. As the light rays pass through the hankie, they bend around the edges of the openings. This causes images to form in several directions. It also makes the images turn with the hankie.

Halo in a hankie
Light a candle and stand some distance away. Stretch a handkerchief and look through it at the candle flame. You see several images of the flame like a halo around the candle. Turn the handkerchief and see how the images turn too.

✹ The light rays from the candle bend as they pass through the tiny openings between the threads of the handkerchief. This causes several images to form.

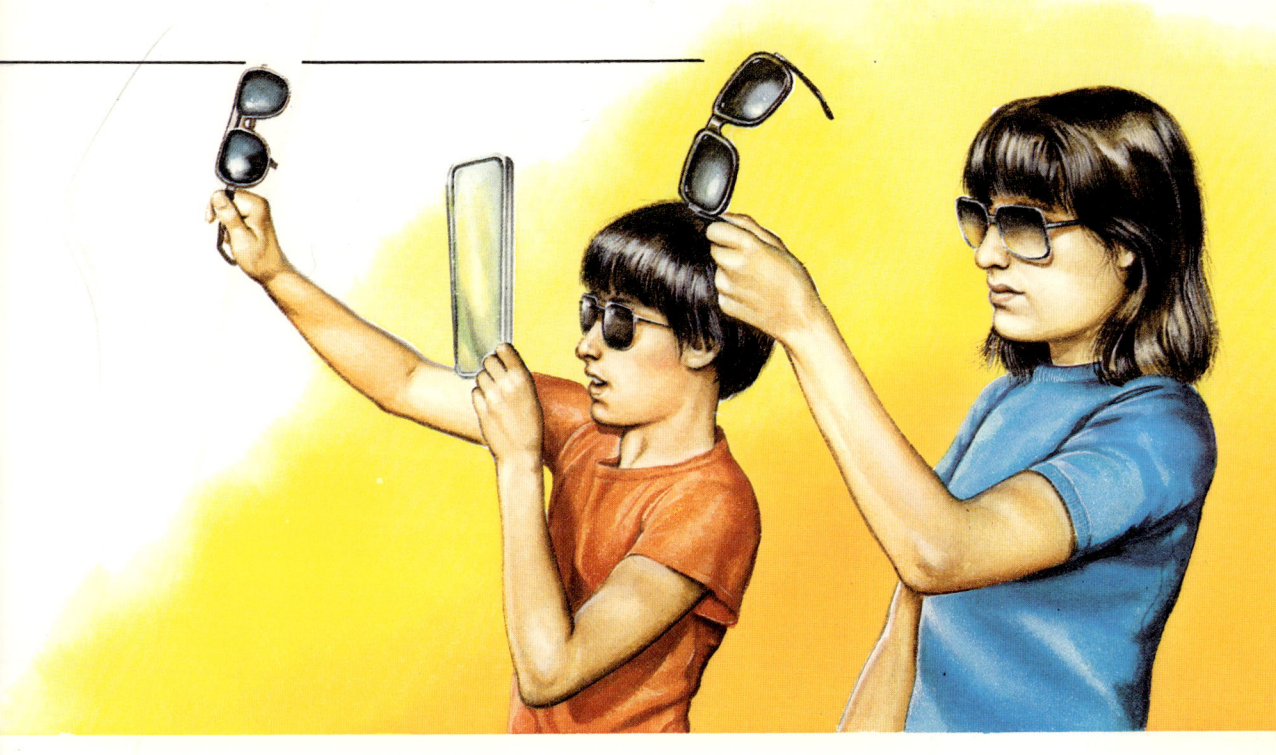

Colors with sunglasses

Take two pairs of sunglasses. They must be polarizing sunglasses that cut out glare. Wear one pair and hold the other pair in front of you. Turn the pair you are holding and see how the lenses go totally dark. Now hold a rigid plastic lid or sheet between the sunglasses. Bright rainbow colors appear in the plastic. Turn the sunglasses and see how the colors change.

※ The sunglasses change light into polarized light. This light may change in color or brightness as it passes through materials.

△ The pair of sunglasses held up produce polarized light. At a certain angle, the pair next to the eyes stop polarized light, which is why the glasses go dark. When the light passes through the plastic, some of the colors in the light are polarized more than others. Certain colors get through the pair of glasses being worn, making colors appear in the plastic.

Glossary

△ A magnifying glass can produce a small image of the Sun on some paper. The light rays that strike the glass are bent so that they meet on the paper and form an image there. The Sun's heat rays meet too, which is why the paper begins to smolder and burn.

Image
We see an object when light rays from it enter our eyes. The rays may first go through a lens or be reflected from a mirror. In this case, we see an image of the object through the lens or in the mirror. The image may be smaller or larger than the object. It may also be upside down, back to front or distorted in shape.

Lens
A lens is a circular piece of glass or plastic with curved sides. It bends the light rays that pass through it from an object. If the light rays then move toward each other, they meet on the other side of the lens. If a surface like a screen is placed at the point where the rays meet, an image of the object is formed on the surface.

Light rays
Light rays are waves of light energy that move out in all directions from a source of light. The source may produce light

because it is very hot, like the Sun, a candle flame or a flashlight bulb. The rays travel in straight lines through the air or any other transparent substance, like glass or water. They light up any object that is not transparent. The rays are reflected from the surface of the object, and we see the object as the rays enter our eyes.

Mirror
A mirror has a very shiny surface behind the glass. You see an image in a mirror because the surface of this layer is very smooth. Light rays from an object are all reflected by the surface toward your eyes. Your brain thinks that the rays have come directly from the object in a straight line, so you see the object as an image in the mirror.

Reflected light
You see a reflection in a smooth surface like a mirror or some water because light rays from a light source or an object bounce off the surface in the same direction. If the surface is rough, light rays are still reflected from it. However, they bounce off at different angles. This makes the object visible but stops it from being shiny like a mirror.

Refraction
Refraction is the bending of light rays that may happen as light goes from one transparent substance to another. The rays always bend toward the denser substance. If they go from water to air, the rays bend toward the water. If they go from air to glass, they bend down into the glass. Refraction does not happen if the rays strike the surface at a right angle. They pass through without bending. Reflection also occurs with refraction. At certain angles, all the light rays may be reflected, without entering the surface at all.

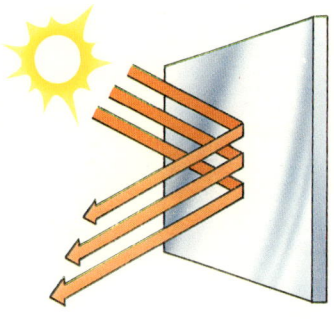

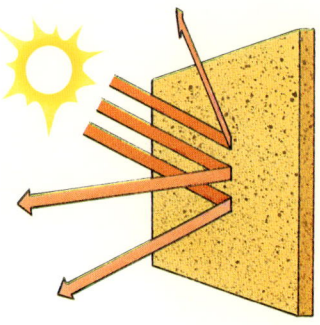

△ A smooth surface like metal reflects rays from a light source in the same direction, which is why it looks shiny. A rough surface like cork reflects the light rays in different directions so that it is not shiny.

Index

air 7, 10, 16, 17, 24

binoculars 6, 19

camera 20, 21
clock 8, 9
color 5, 22, 23, 24, 25, 29
compass 8, 9

diffraction 28

films 21, 26, 27

heat 6
heat rays 7, 30

image 5, 6, 12, 15, 18, 19, 20, 21, 27, 28, 30

kaleidoscope 12

latitude, angle of, 8
lens 5, 17, 18, 19, 20, 21, 29, 30
light 5, 6, 7, 10, 11, 16, 17, 22, 23, 25, 28, 30, 31
light rays 6, 10, 11, 12, 13, 14, 16, 17, 19, 20, 21, 22, 24, 28, 30, 31

magnification 14, 18, 19
magnifying glass 15, 17, 18, 19, 21, 30
microscope 18, 19
mirror 5, 10, 12, 13, 14, 15, 22, 30, 31

paints 23
periscope 13
polarized light 29
projector 20, 21

rainbow 22, 29
rays *see* light rays
reflection 10, 14, 15, 30, 31
refraction 17, 31

spectrum 22
Sun 5, 6, 7, 8, 9, 17, 22, 24, 30, 31
sundial 5, 8
Sun spots 6

telescope 6, 19
television 26, 27
time 5, 8, 9